With warm and special wishes

to _____

from _____

A Mother Knows Just What to Do

illustrated by
michel bernstein

Andrews and McMeel
A Universal Press Syndicate Company
Kansas City

ISBN: 0-8362-4738-8

A
Mother Knows
Just What to Do

When sun isn't sunning
and fun isn't funning
and tea takes
a long time to brew...

When brambles are scratching
or sneezes are catching,
a mother
knows just what to do.

If secrets need sharing
or thoughts need comparing...

...If life is in slight
disarray...

If wee ones need tending
or feelings need mending...
a mother can make life okay!

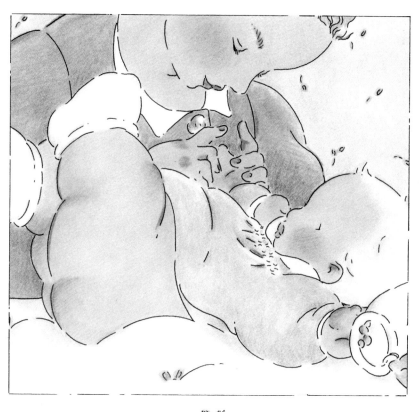

She'll cuddle and kiss you
and talk through the issue,
and suddenly
things are all right...

Where storm clouds of trouble
had started to double,
blue skies are
a welcome delight!

While cooking or sewing
or coming or going,
her children
remain number one—

Her life's such a tizzy
she makes herself dizzy,
but somehow
she gets it all done!

She's patient and kind
when her little ones mind—
There's affection
in each tender look...

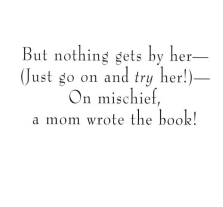

But nothing gets by her—
(Just go on and *try* her!)—
On mischief,
a mom wrote the book!

Ask moms how they do it—
They say, "Nothing to it!"
But everyone
knows it's not true.

That's why there's no other
loved more than a mother
who always knows
just what to do.